EGYPTIAN LIFE

Who Were the Ancient Egyptians?

FIRST INDUSTRY

Smelting, the process of extracting metal ores from rock, was developed in about 4500 B.C. in Egypt and Sumer. The metalworkers above are smelting copper, which was used to make strong tools and weapons.

Sometime around 5000 B.C., loose communities of people began to organize themselves into city-states. These were the first true civilizations. They seem to have sprung up at about the same time in different parts of the world. Yet they grew up independent of each other. All of these early civilizations developed around major river valleys. In China, civilizations formed along the Yellow River. The Indus River, in what is now Pakistan and northwestern India, gave life to the Harappan civilization. The Tigris and Euphrates Rivers in the Middle East formed what was called the Fertile Crescent. From this rich land, the Sumerian culture was born. The Egyptian civilization grew from the banks of the Nile River. Egyptians prayed to the river for life: "Be greeted, Nile, arising here from the earth, come to keep Egypt alive."

THE POTTER'S ART

Before Egyptians invented the potter's wheel, they pressed wet clay by hand. The Nile's black, sticky mud was easy to shape. It dried to a red color.

THE BEGINNINGS OF FARMING

Farming developed at about the same time as settled civilizations. The yearly flooding of the river valleys, including the Nile, left a rich silt on the surrounding land. Egyptians called their land *kemet,* or black land, because of this fertile soil. Others called Egypt the "Gift of the Nile."

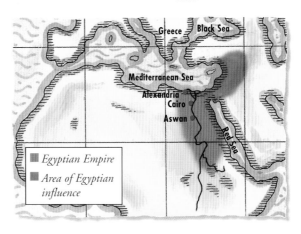

Egyptian Empire

Area of Egyptian influence

A KINGDOM UNITED

At first, Egypt was made up of two kingdoms, Upper and Lower Egypt. They were united about 3100 B.C. Over the next 2,000 years there were three main eras. During the first, the Old Kingdom, the pyramids were built. During the Middle Kingdom, trade was expanded. The New Kingdom saw the addition of new lands.

MONUMENTAL BUILDINGS

Beginning about 2600 B.C., Egyptians built huge stone pyramids. Kings (pharaohs) were buried in them with precious goods to take with them into the afterlife. The Great Pyramid at Giza (shown above) was built about 2551 B.C. It was made of more than 2 million blocks of stone. Each block weighed about 2 1/2 tons. After about 2150 B.C. pyramids were no longer built. Pharaohs were buried in underground tombs.

SIGN OF LIFE

This dish is in the form of an ankh, which is the Egyptian symbol for the breath of life. Mummies were often buried with an ankh.

THE FIRST WRITING

Picture writing first appeared in Sumer, northeast of Egypt, in about 3200 B.C. The Egyptians developed this into a system of writing called hieroglyphs. They used more than 700 symbols to represent various sounds and ideas. Egyptians also had a 24-letter alphabet.

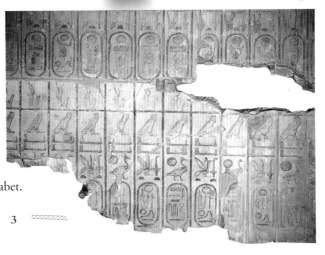

Life for the Rich

ORNATE FURNITURE

Only the wealthy could afford to buy goods made with imported wood. Many furnishings, like this chair, were highly decorated. Women were the owners of all household furniture.

Much of what survives from ancient Egypt forms a picture of great luxury. The homes and the everyday items of the poor were made with materials that have not survived the more than 6,000 years since they were used. The magnificent buildings, art, and artifacts that have survived show the luxury in which royalty, government officials, landowners, nobles, and priests lived. Also, most of the written records focus on concerns of the wealthy. Because of these sources, much is known about the rich in ancient Egypt. For example, some people owned two houses. One was in town, the other was a country home, often fashioned after a royal palace. Comfort and personal cleanliness were an important part of life among the rich. They also had strong family values and saw children as a great joy. Most wealthy families used servants or slaves to carry out the lowly tasks of everyday life.

ARTISTIC GLASS

Egyptians were skilled glassmakers. They also made fine white and color porcelain. Those who could afford them also bought luxury goods from foreign countries. Egyptians were great collectors of such objects. This glass perfume bottle in the shape of a fish might have been one of many decorative fish in a wealthy person's collection.

FINE JEWELRY

Egyptian jewelers were highly skilled. They were especially good at welding thin strips of precious metals together into various shapes. The necklace pictured here shows this technique. Items made of gold and fine jewels, such as turquoise and amethyst, were favorites. Much of the jewelry was also decorated with ceramics and painted glass.

KEEPING UP APPEARANCES

Egyptians, both men and women, took care about their appearance. Among the rich, both sexes wore elaborately braided and decorated wigs.

These were made of wool or human hair, held together with beeswax. Women often wore a cone of perfume on their heads. It would melt when warmed, and its scented oil would drip onto their shoulders.

SPACIOUS HOUSES

The rich had large brick and plaster homes with several stories. They were placed on platforms, like the house at the left in the picture above, to protect them from dampness. The owners lived on the first floor where temperatures were coolest. Household workers did all the cooking in the open air on the flat roof.

COMFORTABLE LIFESTYLE

Houses were comfortably, if simply, furnished. Wealthy Egyptians made great use of rare woods and imported fabrics. Most furniture had detailed carvings, such as lion-claw feet on tables and chairs. Tables were built low. Bed frames were usually made of tightly woven wicker. They had stuffed mattresses for softness. Egyptians also used wooden headrests, like the one shown here, for resting during the day.

Life for the Poor

The plow in this modern picture is much like the one ancient Egyptians used. Peasants worked in teams of two. One flung seeds from a shoulder bag. The other used the plow to cover them up. Land along the Nile was soft enough just after the yearly flooding for this simple plow to work.

There were far more poor people than rich people in ancient Egypt. More than 8 in 10 Egyptians were peasants or laborers. The peasants worked in the fields. The laborers, including slaves, carried out the massive building plans of the pharaohs. These groups were at the bottom of the social scale. As in all classes, a strong family was the basis for happiness. Once children became teenagers they often became servants to richer families. A lucky few of these were able to work their way up into a higher layer of society. Houses for the poor, whether in town or in the country, were made of dried mud mixed with straw and made into bricks. The very poorest among the peasants shared their living space with their farm animals.

GETTING ABOUT

The most common way for the poor to get around was on donkeys. Those better off were able to afford camels or wagons. Travel was difficult because there were few roads. In their whole lives, many people traveled no farther than the local market. Donkeys still provide the main means of transport for poor Egyptians in remote areas.

SIMPLE HOUSING

This clay model shows a typical poor Egyptian's house. It has an arched doorway and small windows to keep out heat. Clay models like this were buried with their owners for use in the next life.

A MEASURE OF WEALTH

Many farmers dreaded the yearly arrival of the government officials. This is because the farmers learned what they owed the government in taxes. One measure of wealth was the number of farm animals owned, especially cattle. Officials brought rolls of string which they unwound like a tape measure to determine the size of a farmer's fields. Scribes recorded the details, and the farmers were taxed accordingly. Before the use of money, farmers paid their taxes with a portion of their crops or with other items.

HARD LABOR

This wall painting from a tomb in Thebes is more than 3,000 years old. The plow is almost the same as the one at the top of page 6. The plowman is using a whip, made from papyrus, to swat flies and drive on the ox. Wives often worked alongside their husbands.

SLAVE TRADE

Like most ancient civilizations, Egypt relied on slaves to carry out their daily tasks. Most came from other lands, such as Nubia, Ethiopia, or Lebanon, where Egypt extended its rule. Some were put to work as servants for the wealthy. Most, however, served among the huge ranks of workers that built the magnificent pyramids and other structures. The unskilled were put to work in the fields during sowing time.

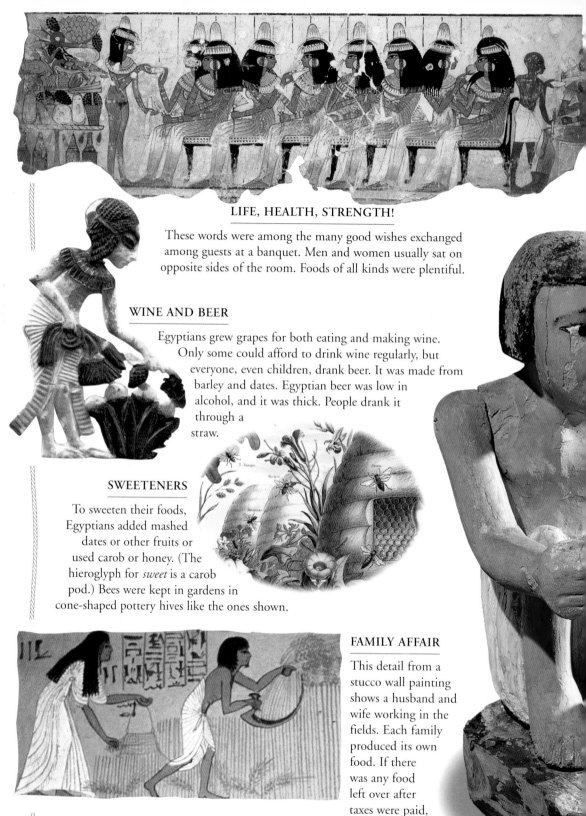

LIFE, HEALTH, STRENGTH!

These words were among the many good wishes exchanged among guests at a banquet. Men and women usually sat on opposite sides of the room. Foods of all kinds were plentiful.

WINE AND BEER

Egyptians grew grapes for both eating and making wine. Only some could afford to drink wine regularly, but everyone, even children, drank beer. It was made from barley and dates. Egyptian beer was low in alcohol, and it was thick. People drank it through a straw.

SWEETENERS

To sweeten their foods, Egyptians added mashed dates or other fruits or used carob or honey. (The hieroglyph for *sweet* is a carob pod.) Bees were kept in gardens in cone-shaped pottery hives like the ones shown.

FAMILY AFFAIR

This detail from a stucco wall painting shows a husband and wife working in the fields. Each family produced its own food. If there was any food left over after taxes were paid, farmers took it to the local market. The Egyptians are believed to have invented the first ox-drawn plow in about 3100 B.C.

Food & Drink

Most Egyptians had enough to eat. But they never took their food supply for granted. If the Nile flooded too much or not enough, they might have a hungry year. Insects sometimes destroyed crops. Most of the time, however, Egyptians enjoyed a wide variety of foods. Their diets included various meats (farmed or hunted) and fish from the Nile. Egyptians also bred chickens to ensure plentiful supplies of poultry. They had plenty of vegetables, including onions, leeks, turnips, and garlic. Garlic was so well liked it was sometimes buried in tombs for the afterlife. Fruits, including grapes, figs, dates, and pomegranates, were also in good supply. Wine was a great favorite, especially among the rich. It was stored in pottery jars that were sealed with lumps of clay. Egyptians of all classes took great pleasure in their food and drink. Hosts of banquets tried to feed their guests as well as they could afford. They believed that doing so would assure the admiration of others and win the praise of the gods.

THE BUTCHER'S TRADE

Wealthy Egyptians enjoyed a variety of meats, including sheep, oxen, and poultry. They also hunted wild animals, such as the antelope shown here, for meat. Animals were also sacrificed to the gods. Butchers followed a strict ritual for presenting the offering.

OPEN HEARTHS

Cooking was usually done in clay ovens or over open charcoal fires, as shown here. Firewood was in short supply, and fires were tended carefully. The boy in this wooden sculpture is fanning a fire. He is preparing to cook the duck he is holding.

STAFF OF LIFE

Bread formed the staple diet of many Egyptians. In fact, Egyptians had as many as 15 different words for bread. Bread was made from barley and wheat. It was baked in round covered molds. This picture shows an official measuring a wheat field.

Pastimes

E gyptians spent a good portion of their lives enjoying pastimes. In contrast to some other ancient civilizations, Egyptians had few large-scale public entertainments. There were no stadiums, for example, where people might have gathered to watch sporting events. There were, however, yearly religious ceremonies in which whole communities took part. In general, Egyptians passed their time in individual or family activities. They loved dining, music, dancing, athletics, board games, storytelling, and hunting. In contrast to customs in other ancient cultures, Egyptian men and women enjoyed pastimes together, usually as equals. Each class of people had some time to spend in pleasant pastimes. But the wealthy had the time and money to pursue their pleasures in grand style.

PHYSICALLY FIT

This carving of two young men boxing comes from the temple of Ramses III. Egyptians valued the health benefits of active exercise. Other popular sports were wrestling, gymnastics, and jousting from boats.

GYPSIES

Modern-day gypsies may be descendants of Egyptians who fled their homeland when the Greeks gained control. Many traditional gypsy pastimes, such as horse racing and group singing and dancing, might also have been practiced in ancient Egypt.

SKILLED DANCERS

No banquet of the royal or wealthy was complete without song and dance. Servant girls who had completed challenging training in dance performed for the guests. Gymnasts and jugglers also performed, often to the music of flutes, harps, and cymbals.

THE FIRST HARP

Egyptians may have invented the harp (shown at the left) sometime around 3100 B.C. Harps came in all sizes. Some were taller than their players. Egyptian music often had a lively beat. Listeners snapped their fingers or clapped their hands to the rhythm of the music.

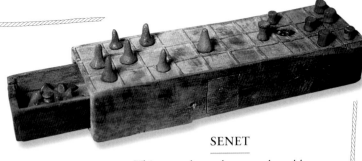

SENET

This carved wooden senet board has a drawer to store the playing pieces. It dates from about 1200 B.C. A senet board made of ebony and ivory was found in the tomb of Tutankhamen.

BOARD GAMES

The most popular Egyptian game was senet. Two players tried to reach the kingdom of the gods by advancing their pieces. The senet game board at the left was drawn onto a papyrus sheet. Another popular game was Hounds and Jackals. Pegs in the shapes of these animals were moved from hole to hole across a board. Instead of throwing dice, Egyptians tossed sticks to determine their moves.

FAMILY VALUES

Egyptian society, at all levels, valued families and children. For wealthy Egyptians, an afternoon of family hunting for sport was one of the best ways to pass time together. Egyptians were also great storytellers. Elders and children, males and females, all delighted in hearing the stories of the gods' heroic deeds.

WIGS AND HEADDRESSES

Both men and women wore their hair short or shaved their heads and wore wigs. Headdresses were worn for special purposes.

Headdresses might take the form of elaborate hats or resemble wigs with finely braided hair. Often these were decorated with jewels. For the poorer classes, working in the fierce Egyptian sun, skull caps or bonnets were worn.

Fashion

gyptians valued personal cleanliness and good looks. They washed several times a day. The rich spent time each morning with servants who cut and shaped their hair, trimmed their nails and softened their hands, and applied scented oils to their skin. Poorer people used barbers who set up shop in the open air. As they waited their turn under the trees they could catch up with their neighbors on the latest news. Both men and women, even the poor, wore jewelry and eye makeup. Because of the hot climate, most clothes were simple, light, and loose fitting. Men usually wore short kilts. Women wore simple skirts or long pleated dresses that were wrapped around the body. Children up to age 12 sometimes wore nothing at all.

HAIRDRESSERS' TOOLS

Wigs and hair extensions were joined to the head with hairpins made of wood or bone. Combs with fine teeth were made of wood or, as shown here, ivory. The finely braided hairstyles of the wigs took care and skill to create.

FOOTWEAR

When people were not going barefoot, they wore simple sandals with a thong between the toes. Most sandals were made of woven papyrus reeds. This picture shows men making papyrus. Footwear was also made of leather. A few of the very wealthy even owned sandals made of gold.

VÉRITABLE EXTRAIT DE VIANDE LIEBIG.

Histoire du papier. 2.
Fabricants de papier égyptiens.

EYE WEAR

Makeup was widely used by men and women and helped protect the eyes from the sun. It was kept in fancy containers like the one above. Minerals were ground up to form pastes. Green eye makeup, made from malachite, was the most popular.

STUNNING JEWELRY

Poor people wore jewelry made of cheap metals or shells. These were often decorated with pieces of brightly painted clay. The wealthy wore gold and precious stones. Some wore jeweled braids that hung from a headband around the forehead. Egyptian jewelers were highly skilled with metal. The gold and lapis lazuli necklace (left) and chest ornament (right) are from Tutankhamen's tomb.

LINEN FOR COOLNESS

Clothing for men and women was often made from linen. The fabric was light, airy, and very finely woven. This 5,000-year-old garment may be the oldest surviving piece of clothing in the world.

Art & Architecture

The Egyptians made many advances in architecture. For example, they may have been the first culture to use stone as a building material. They also built some of the biggest structures in the ancient world, the pyramids. These were burial places for the pharaohs. In the earliest days, graves were just holes in the sand. Later graves had mounds of sand added on top. Before long, flat, single-story rectangular tombs were built with mud bricks. In time, more and more layers were added, each one slightly smaller than the one it rested on. These layers made step pyramids that reached to the sky. The last pyramids to be built were true pyramids—smooth-sided, not stepped. Temples to the gods were also impressive buildings. Usually there were huge carved statues, often of the pharaohs, at their entrances. Both the pyramids and the huge carvings required precise planning and design. The statues were just one kind of fine art that the ancient Egyptians created. They also made colorful wall paintings drawn with precise measurements. Egyptian pottery and jewelry were also skillfully crafted.

MONUMENTAL ART

This picture shows part of a huge statue of King Ramses II at Luxor. It was carved from a single piece of stone, the largest ever seen in Egypt. Ramses himself was present at the quarry when the stone was uncovered. The quarry workers believed the pharaoh's presence had created it. Within a year, well-paid workers had turned the huge slab into a colossal statue of Ramses.

DRAWING AND WRITING

Drawing and writing w[ere] much alike to Egyptian[s]. Their paintings and wa[ll] carvings, like their hieroglyphs, all told stories. Artists showed t[he] ideal, not real, appearan[ce] of their subjects.

TEMPLE AT ABU SIMBEL

Ramses II ruled Egypt for more than 60 years. At Abu Simbel, in the Upper Nile, he built a temple into the side of a cliff. The temple was dedicated to himself and to the god Amun-Re. It was positioned so that sunlight would flood into it twice a year, on the first day of spring and the first day of fall. Four huge statues of Ramses guard the entrance.

OBELISKS

Obelisks are tall, pointed pillars carved from single blocks of stone. They usually stood in pairs at the entrances of temples or tombs.
Hieroglyphs carved on their sides told who built them and to which god they were dedicated. This one, and the statues (left) of Ramses II, are at Luxor.

THE GREAT HALL

This picture shows a great hall inside the temple at Karnak, built by Ramses II. The hall was roofed in slabs of stone supported by pillars. It was very dark inside. Light came in from windows with vertical bars (top center).

THE PYRAMIDS

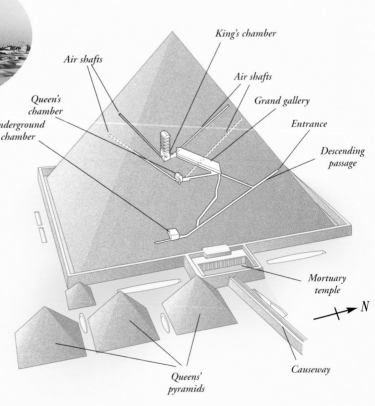

The great pyramids of Giza were built as tombs for mighty Egyptian pharaohs. The Great Pyramid (right) was built around 2551 B.C. for King Khufu. It stands 481 feet (146.6 m) high. It is made from about 2,300,000 blocks of stone, each weighing more than two tons. It was so carefully built that the base is level to within less than 1 inch (2.1 cm). Pharaohs put their soldiers to work on these huge projects. Egyptians were seldom at war. So the soldiers were free to labor on these building projects.

King's chamber

Air shafts

Air shafts

Queen's chamber

Grand gallery

Underground chamber

Entrance

Descending passage

Mortuary temple

N

Queens' pyramids

Causeway

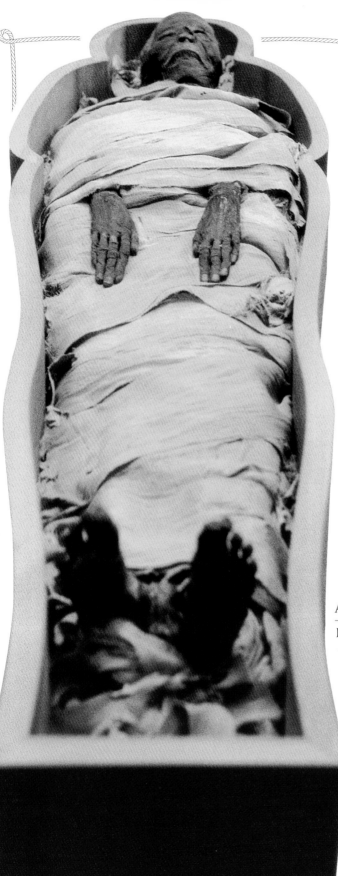

EMBALMING

Embalmers prepared mummies. Before wrapping the body, they took out the organs. The brain came out through the nose. Then the organs were placed in jars. Spells were carved on the jars to allow the organs to return to the body in the next world.

DOCTOR PRIESTS

The temple at Edfou (above) was one of many temples where people could go for treatment. In early times, Egyptians thought evil spirits caused disease. For this reason, only priests were allowed to cure the sick. Later, doctors were trained in the science of healing.

ANIMAL STUDIES

Egyptians believed in an afterlife. So doctors were not allowed to dissect human corpses. Instead, they learned about the inner workings of bodies from animals. They understood that the heart was the center of the blood system. They also knew the function of the major organs, including the brain.

Health & Medicine

The medical practices of the Egyptians were a mix of science and magic. Egyptians understood certain workings of the human body, including the flow of blood. But from their experience in butchering they knew more about animals' bodies than humans'. In fact, wall art sometimes shows the organs of animals drawn inside humans. Egyptians knew how to set a broken bone in a splint so it would heal properly. They used herbs, especially garlic, as a cure for some common illnesses. But magic was also often part of the remedy, or even the whole prescription. For example, a person suffering from headaches might have been told to pray over a clay figure of a crocodile with a seed in its mouth. Much of the healing rituals took place at temples. The sick brought offerings to the gods to aid the healing process. Doctors trained in temples, in an area called the House of Life. The average life span was 30–35 years.

DENTISTRY

This carving from about 2700 B.C. shows a king's chief dentist and doctor. Studies of mummies show that Egyptians had good dental skills. They knew how to fill cavities. They also made gold bridges between teeth.

SPREAD OF GERMS

Many viruses pass from hand to hand. Others are carried by flies or other insects from one person to another. Keeping clean was and is a good way to prevent the spread of germs. Priests followed strict rules for cleanliness. They washed their hands often and kept their heads shaved.

LOTUS MAGIC

The lotus flower was an important symbol to the Egyptians. They believed the sun god had been born in a lotus flower. The scent of the sacred lotus flower was thought to guard against disease.

Love & Marriage

ALL IN THE FAMILY

There is some evidence to suggest that marriage between relatives was sometimes allowed in ancient Egypt, usually among royalty. In religion, the earth god Geb (above) married his sister Nut, the sky goddess.

In many ancient cultures, young people had little if any choice about whom they married. In Egypt, girls by law had the right to choose their marriage partners. In fact, however, most marriages were arranged by families to increase wealth. Girls married as early as age 12. Boys were usually a bit older. There was no formal legal ceremony for marriage. Instead, two people had to consent to a marriage. The family usually held a big feast. Many gifts were offered, especially those to help with setting up a household. If a groom could afford it, he might give his new wife a slave. Married men had to provide for their families. The care of children and the elderly was the job of women. Love poetry from ancient Egypt shows that men and women deeply enjoyed each other's love. In one poem, a young man pretends to be sick to get his true love to come to his side. In another, only the flooding Nile can keep the lovers apart.

GODDESS OF FERTILITY

The Egyptian goddess of fertility was Taweret. She was usually shown as a pregnant creature. She had the face of a hippo, legs and feet of a lion, and a headdress like a crocodile's tail. She usually wore a fierce look on her face to keep evil away during childbirth. Women said prayers and made offerings to her when expecting babies. Women had many children. A woman might spend eight or more years of her life being pregnant.

FAMILY VIRTUES

Ancient Egypt was a gentle culture. The people observed many social graces. Single girls of high rank had chaperones when meeting men. On the whole, men were respectful of women. In other ancient cultures, women were kept separate from the men, sometimes living in different parts of the house. In Egypt, families liked to be together.

GIRL POWER

Wives of important nobles held considerable power behind the scenes. Wives at court would sometimes gather together under the protection of the goddess Hathar. They would together ask their husbands to take a certain action that they supported. They often won their cases. The couple at left were no doubt among the noble class. Only the wealthy could afford such heavy headdresses.

DEVOTED COUPLE

Most Egyptian couples remained married for life. Women had the same right as men to request a divorce. In the case of a divorce, women kept what property they had at the beginning of the marriage. They also were allowed to take a third of the joint property. Being married was part of an Egyptian's idea of happiness. Marriage led to children, and children were the greatest possible blessing.

WEDDING CEREMONY

This painting from the tomb of Sennufer, mayor of Thebes, portrays his marriage to Meryt, a musician in the temple of Amun. They are being blessed with holy water. Other paintings show the couple lovingly touching one another's shoulders and hands. Wives and husbands expected to meet again in the afterlife.

Women & Children

The blessings of the Nile and the mild climate gave Egyptians an easy life compared to that of other ancient cultures. Since they could grow as much food as they needed, Egyptians might feed large families. In other ancient cultures, unwanted babies could be left to die. In Egypt, all babies were wanted, although sons were considered a special blessing. In most families, it was the women's job to look after the house, care for the children, and cook and clean. Women also cared for the sick in their families. They used herbs to make cures, prayed to the gods, and called in a doctor when needed. Rich women usually had slaves or servants do this work for them.

CHILDREN'S GAMES

These carvings show children carrying models in the shape of birds. They floated these on water like boats. Some modern games may have had their start in ancient Egypt. Children played games like leap-frog, piggyback, and tug-of-war.

WEAVING, SEWING, WASHING

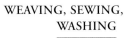

Women made and washed their family's clothes. They even wove the linen from which the clothes were made. If they had any cloth left after making their family's clothes, they could trade it at the market for other needed goods.

CLEOPATRA

Cleopatra VII (above center) was the last in the long line of rulers of Egypt. At first she shared the rule with her father and then with her brothers. In 48 B.C., the Roman general Julius Caesar invaded Egypt. Cleopatra married a Roman commander named Mark Antony and together they challenged the rule of Caesar. Led by Octavius, Caesar's army defeated the troops of Antony and Cleopatra in A.D. 30. Rather than face defeat, Antony and Cleopatra took their own lives. Egypt became a province of Rome.

QUEEN NEFERTITI

Queen Nefertiti ruled with her husband, Akhenaten. She lived up to her name, which means "the beautiful woman has come." She is often shown standing with her husband as an equal. Neither she nor her husband were well liked. They banned the worship of old gods and claimed that Akhenaten was the son of the sun god. Tutankhamen later restored the gods to favor.

FAMILY TASKS

Women often worked while holding their children in a kind of papoose. As soon as they were able, children would help with the chores.

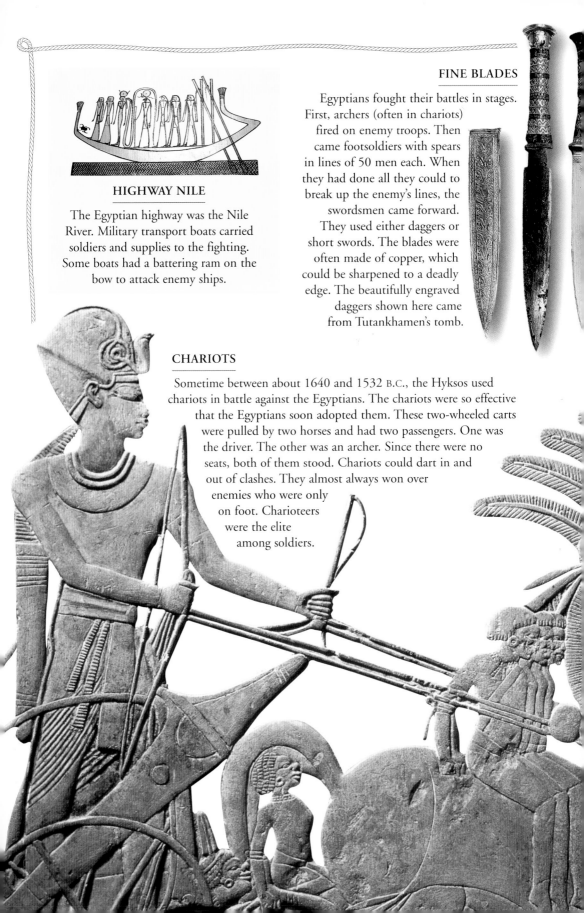

HIGHWAY NILE

The Egyptian highway was the Nile River. Military transport boats carried soldiers and supplies to the fighting. Some boats had a battering ram on the bow to attack enemy ships.

FINE BLADES

Egyptians fought their battles in stages. First, archers (often in chariots) fired on enemy troops. Then came footsoldiers with spears in lines of 50 men each. When they had done all they could to break up the enemy's lines, the swordsmen came forward. They used either daggers or short swords. The blades were often made of copper, which could be sharpened to a deadly edge. The beautifully engraved daggers shown here came from Tutankhamen's tomb.

CHARIOTS

Sometime between about 1640 and 1532 B.C., the Hyksos used chariots in battle against the Egyptians. The chariots were so effective that the Egyptians soon adopted them. These two-wheeled carts were pulled by two horses and had two passengers. One was the driver. The other was an archer. Since there were no seats, both of them stood. Chariots could dart in and out of clashes. They almost always won over enemies who were only on foot. Charioteers were the elite among soldiers.

War & Weaponry

Between the years 5000 and 3100 B.C. there were two separate Egyptian kingdoms, Upper and Lower Egypt. In those years, fighting was rare. It often took place among poorly organized bands of people. In about 3100 B.C., King Menes united the two kingdoms. The years following were also generally peaceful. When pharaohs needed soldiers, they would enlist farmers to serve. Later, during the New Kingdom (about 1550–1070 B.C.), Egypt began to extend its rule beyond the Nile valley, from Nubia in the south to Sumer and Syria in the north. Since the Nile's resources were plentiful, there was little reason for Egyptians to fight one another. But Egypt's richness often attracted the greedy attention of other nations. Egypt took a hard stand against those who tried to invade. Pharaohs organized effective armies of archers, charioteers, and footsoldiers. Pharaohs themselves would often take the lead in major battles. In time, though, Egypt fell after multiple invasions.

ROYAL WARRIORS

This picture shows Pharaoh Ramses II in battle, overcoming his enemies. One account says this about the Pharaoh's fighting. "His Majesty slaughtered them in their places. They sprawled before his horses." Nefertiti, wife of King Akhenaten, may also have gone into battle with her husband.

BRONZE IN BATTLE

Egypt did not develop advanced weapons on its own. Enemies with better weapons, such as the Hyksos, had the upper hand. After clashing with the Hyksos, Egyptians copied their strong bronze weapons and their style of armor and helmets.

MILITARY POMP

At the start of a war, soldiers would receive their weapons, with the Pharaoh himself present in his glittering royal outfit. Wars were fought with great pomp and ceremony. A troop of trumpeters marched along with the army. The pharaoh's chariot was decorated with a ram's head and a symbol of the sun to represent Amun-Re. Figures of other gods, including that of the moon god, Khansu, shown here, might also go along.

Crime & Punishment

Egyptian laws were strict and their punishments harsh. Those guilty of forgery (signing someone else's name) had their hands cut off. Talking about the overthrow of the pharaoh was punished by removing the offender's tongue. Pregnant women who had committed a crime were punished only after they had given birth. A soldier guilty of any crime had to make amends by performing a heroic deed. A woman who was unfaithful to her husband might have her nose cut off. It was everyone's duty to prevent or report crimes, or to go to someone's aid if they were in danger. Pharaohs believed that if citizens were properly protected against crime, their good feelings would reflect on society itself. One of the most common crimes in ancient Egypt was stealing the riches placed in the tombs of long-dead pharaohs. The first known looting of a tomb occurred in about 1100 B.C. Tombs carried warnings to looters about the anger and revenge of the gods.

MAKING MONEY

Egyptians began to use coins for money about 300 B.C. Before that, Egyptians traded goods of equal value. Anyone found guilty of making fake coins had their hands cut off. The gold coin shown here is from Cleopatra's time (about A.D. 40).

ALL-SEEING GOD

According to legends, Osiris, the god of the dead, was once the pharaoh. His jealous brother Seth, god of storms and war, killed him and cut his body into pieces. Isis, wife of Osiris, found the pieces and put them back together. They had a son, Horus, god of the day and air. This all-seeing god protected the citizens of Egypt. He would make sure that unpunished crimes of the living would be judged again in death.

SLAVE TRADE

This carving from the temple of Ramses III shows defeated soldiers taken into slavery. They are led by a rope tied around their necks. Slaves who tried to escape often had one hand cut off so they could not try again. Slaves and prisoners did much of the work on the pharaohs' building programs. Many died in this dangerous work.

CITIZEN'S DUTY

Egyptian society was largely self-policing. That is, every citizen had the power to accuse and prosecute a criminal. Failing to do so was itself a crime. Witnesses who did not fulfill their duty were beaten with branches.

LAW OF DECLARATION

Bakers (above), shepherds, scribes—everyone had to provide a written report to the government describing his job. Those who could not tell the government how they earned a living legally were assumed to be breaking the law. The punishment was death.

HEARTS AND FEATHERS

Egyptians believed that the dead had to be judged before reaching paradise. The goddess of truth, Maat, would place a feather in a scale. The person's heart would be placed on the other side of the balance. If the heart did not balance with the feather, eternal life was denied. The godly scribe Thoth would record the results. Thoth is shown here as a baboon trying to catch a thief.

Transport & Science

Ancient Egyptians lived a comfortable life on the whole. They were generally content to continue to do things as they had been done for ages. So there was little push toward inventing new methods and new tools. Nonetheless, the Egyptians did make the world's first potter's wheel. This tool, which is still used, allowed potters to make many kinds of objects. Egyptians made the most of the resources they found around them. Their monuments show their skill at building with stone.

Their buildings also show their skill as architects. They made great use of papyrus, a tall reed that grew along the Nile. They made everything from paper to boats out of this plant. In the sciences, Egyptians had a good knowledge of plants and animals. They knew the size of the earth, and they used a kind of decimal system in their mathematics. They studied the sky and created accurate calendars.

RIDING IN STYLE

An important person would travel around the city in a canopied chair that servants carried by two poles at the bottom. To keep themselves going, the servants would chant: "We would rather carry it full than empty."

CHARTING TIME

From studying the movements of heavenly bodies, Egyptian priests devised a yearly calendar of 365 days. They grouped the days into 12 equal months of 30 days, with 5 days left over. They divided days into hours and used sundials and water clocks to mark time.

WHEELED VEHICLES

Sumerians probably made the world's first wheeled vehicles about 5,000 years ago. Egyptians copied them and made many types of wheeled vehicles. None survive, however. (The one shown above is from the 9th century A.D.)

THE SKY GOD

The Egyptians saw the study of the heavens as the duty of priests. So the priests were also astronomers. Egyptian priests identified five planets and understood their orbiting motions. They also tried to explain heavenly events with religion. For example, they believed Nut, goddess of the sky, caused night by coming down from the sky and visiting her husband Geb (god of the earth). They also thought she caused eclipses by stealing away to see her husband sometimes during the day.

REED BOATS

Wood was scarce in Egypt, so many boats were made of papyrus. Boat makers would bundle the cut papyrus tightly and then strap it to a frame. Several layers together made the boat waterproof. Many of these boats were steered with long forked poles. Fishing trips sometimes began with a game of trying to tip one another's boats. It was all in good fun.

MAKING PAPER

Flat strips of papyrus were pounded together in layers to make a strong paper. The sap acted like a glue, bonding the strips into one sheet. Papyrus sheets could be cleaned and used again.

RIVER TRANSPORT

This model, found in a tomb, is probably like many of the boats that sailed the Nile. River travel was far more common than travel by road. But Egyptians did maintain roads along the canals they dug.

THOTH

Thoth, god of the moon, was believed to be the intelligence of the universe. He is given credit for teaching people language, writing, art, music, architecture, and mathematics. He is often shown as an ibis, a bird whose curved beak looks like the crescent moon. Thoth also sometimes took the form of a baboon.

ANUBIS

Anubis was the god of embalming and the god of the cemetery. His animal symbol was the jackal. The priest shown here, wearing a jackal mask, is performing the Opening of the Mouth ceremony on the dead during the mummification process. The open mouth was thought to allow the person's soul to escape and begin its journey to the afterlife.

THE SPHINX

This giant monument at Giza is on the beginning of the road to the pyramid where King Khafre was buried. It has the body of a crouching lion and the face of Khafre himself. It was carved from solid rock in about 2500 B.C. It may have been built to stand guard for the tomb of Khafre.

BOOKS OF THE DEAD

Ancient Egyptians saw death as a phase between this life and the afterlife. They expected their lives after death to be even better than their lives on earth. Books of the Dead (detail from one shown right) were buried with the bodies. The dead were to recite magical spells from the book to ensure safe passage to the next life.

Religion

The he religion of the Egyptians may seem complex. There were hundreds of different gods and goddesses, many who took the form of animals. (Sometimes priests would wear an animal mask to make people think they were the actual god.) However, the final wishes of Ramses III showed fairly simple hopes. He asked the gods for happiness in death and a long reign for his son, filled with honor and blessed with Nile floods. The ancient Egyptians kept many libraries of books, mostly of sacred writings. Many talk about an afterlife. The dead traveled on a long and difficult journey through the underworld. The spirit had to overcome many obstacles. To aid them in their journey, bodies were mummified (or preserved). Buried with them were books and carvings of magic spells to ward off the evils they would meet. At the end of the journey, the goodness of their hearts would be tested. An evil demon would eat up those who failed the test.

THE TEMPLE OF KARNAK

The magnificent temple at Karnak was begun between 1504–1592 B.C. The temple, like many others, was dedicated to Amun-Re, protector of the pharaohs. He came into being when a local god, Amun, became popular. Rather than unseat the old god, Re, leaders combined the two gods and created Amun-Re. He was the "one true god" of the New Kingdom.

THE SACRED THREE

Egyptians believed in a three-in-one god, Amun-Re. He was made of Amun (the father), Mouth (the mother), and Khons (the son), shown in the middle above.

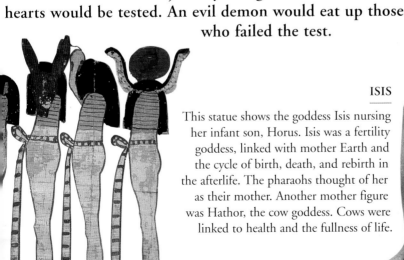

ISIS

This statue shows the goddess Isis nursing her infant son, Horus. Isis was a fertility goddess, linked with mother Earth and the cycle of birth, death, and rebirth in the afterlife. The pharaohs thought of her as their mother. Another mother figure was Hathor, the cow goddess. Cows were linked to health and the fullness of life.

Legacy of the Past

The towering pyramids at Giza stand only a short distance from modern-day Cairo (below). Their glory is a lasting reminder of one of the greatest civilizations of the ancient world. Egypt's monumental architecture is one of its most important legacies. The ancient Greeks were much influenced by Egyptian accomplishments, especially in medicine and science. The Greeks, in turn, influenced the Romans, whose ideas still shape modern life. The ancient Egyptians are also believed to have created the week as a unit of time. They named the days after the sun, the moon, and the five planets they had identified. Egyptian art shows the people's great love for life and for their families. Their poetry echoes with images and ideas that are still fresh.

TUTANKHAMEN'S TREASURE

Tutankhamen was only 18 years old when he died about 1344 B.C. But he has played a remarkable role in revealing the history of Egypt. His tomb, opened in 1922, is the only known tomb of a pharaoh to have escaped looting. The fabulous jewelry, artifacts, and art buried with him have given the modern world an unmatched glimpse of ancient Egypt. His burial mask, above, was made from gold, inlaid with the precious blue stone lapus lazuli. Treasures from the tomb have been displayed around the world.

WRITTEN IN THE STARS

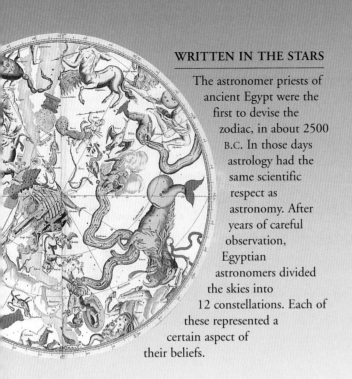

The astronomer priests of ancient Egypt were the first to devise the zodiac, in about 2500 B.C. In those days astrology had the same scientific respect as astronomy. After years of careful observation, Egyptian astronomers divided the skies into 12 constellations. Each of these represented a certain aspect of their beliefs.

architrave *capital*

UNIQUE ARCHITECTURE

Egyptian architecture is different in many ways from European building styles. Cultures with a similar style are those of the Aztec and Inca of Central and South America. One striking feature of Egyptian buildings is their use of irregularly shaped and accurate stone joints. Another is the style of columns. Square blocks on top of the capitals support the architrave above.

THE POTTER'S WHEEL

One of the most enduring gifts from ancient Egypt is the potter's wheel. It was invented around 4000 B.C. It allowed elaborate pieces of pottery to be mass-produced for the first time. Potter's wheels today, like those of ancient Egypt, are operated by a simple foot control.

DID YOU KNOW?

That the Egyptians first used aromatherapy?
Many modern forms of medicine have their origins in the distant past. Aromatherapy, for instance, was first used by the ancient Egyptians to cure many stress-related, respiratory, and muscular ailments. Powerful aromas, extracted from plants, were used to calm the patient's state of mind. This allowed the gods to cure them. Modern doctors are beginning to appreciate the benefits of aromatherapy in treating the same kinds of ailments.

That the Egyptians were the first to study astronomy? Humans have always observed and cataloged natural phenomena such as the seasons, and governed their lives accordingly. By using their knowledge of mathematics, the ancient Egyptians discovered that certain events like eclipses were repeated on a regular basis. They found that they could predict these events with accuracy. These discoveries became part of their religious rituals. For example, they observed that Sirius, the dog star, appeared at a precise location immediately before the annual flooding of the Nile. This event was celebrated by priests in a fertility ceremony.

That the tombs of the pharaohs were protected by a curse? To protect the dead pharaohs and their possessions in their journey to the afterlife, their tombs were protected by a curse. It said that anyone who spoiled their tombs would die. Coincidentally, following the discovery of Tutankhamen's tomb in 1922,

several of those involved died violent deaths, including Lord Carnarvon, who paid for the expedition. He died from an infected mosquito bite five months later. However, archaeologists have detected traces of poisons painted onto the walls of tombs, which, in some cases, may have helped the curse to come true!

That the temples of Abu Simbel were rebuilt in modern times? In the 1960s it was decided to build a massive dam on the Nile at Aswan to relieve Egypt's water shortages. Unfortunately, several important archaeological sites would have been flooded in the process. Among them would have been the temples of Queen Nefertari and Ramses II at Abu Simbel. An international rescue bid was mounted. The huge temples and statues were carefully dismantled. The pieces were numbered and then carefully reconstructed about 750 feet away, safely above the water line.

That the Egyptians may have invented zero in mathematics? Zero behaves differently from other numbers: it is not used in counting; if multiplied by any other number, the answer is always zero; if added to the right of any number, that number increases by 10. The Egyptians first recognized the need to express zero when making up their accounts. They found it useful to show the answer when subtracting two equal amounts from one another.

ACKNOWLEDGMENTS

Map of the World: David Hobbs Picture Research: Image Select
Published by Jamestown Publishers, a division of NTC/Contemporary Publishing Group, Inc.
4255 West Touhy Avenue Lincolnwood (Chicago), Illinois 60712-1975, U.S.A.
This edition © 2001 by NTC/Contemporary Publishing Group, Inc. ISBN: 0-8092-9594-6
First published in Great Britain in 1998 by ticktock Publishing Ltd., The Offices in the Square, Hadlow, Tonbridge, Kent, TN110DD.
© 1998 ticktock Publishing Ltd. All rights reserved.
No part of this publication may be reproduced, stored in a retrieval system, or transmitted in any form or by any means without the prior written permission of the publisher. Printed in Hong Kong.

Picture Credits:
t=top, b=bottom, c=center, l=left, r=right, IFC=inside front cover, OFC=outside front cover

AKG; 27tr. Ancient Art and Architecture; 4tl, 10br, 11tr, 17br, 19br, 21br, 20/21ct, 22tr, 23br, 24tl, 30tl & OFC. Ann Ronan at Image Select; 7r, 8t, 8c, 13tr, 15c, 16l, 18/19c. Chris Fairclough Colour Library /Image Select; 2/3ct, 6bl, 14/15ct, 16cr. et archive; 7bl, 10/11c, 16/17ct, 22b, 28/29cb. Giraudon; 29tr. Image Select; 10bl, 13bl, 14tl & OFC, 21c & 32c & OFC, 27cr, 28c. National Maritime Museum, London; 31tl. PIX; 2bl, 3cl & OFC, 6/7c, 15tr, 15cl, 20tl, 20bl, 22tl, 23cb, 24bl, 28/29ct, 31tr. Spectrum Colour Library; 20br, 27br, 31l, 30/31(main pic). Werner Forman Archive; 2tr, 3cr, 3br, 4bl, 5br, 5tr, 5c, 4/5c & OFC, 7tr, 8l, 8bl, 9tr, 9br, 8/9c, 10tl, 10/11cb, 11br, 12br, 12l, 13br, 13c, 13cr, 14bl, 16/17cb, 17tr, 18tl & OFC, 18bl, 19c, 19tr, 23tr, 24/25c, 25t, 25br, 26tl, 26bl, 26/27c, 28l, 28r & OFC.

Every effort has been made to trace the copyright holders and we apologize in advance for any unintentional omissions. We would be pleased to insert the appropriate acknowledgment in any subsequent edition of this publication.